Be More Cloud

Rediscover your authentic self

through the healing power of nature

Danny Lawson

ISBN: 978-1-3999-2536-5

FOR CHÉRIE

CONTENTS

1 THE TIME BEFORE

As a young girl of five or six years old, B discovered that she already had the ability to transcend her own physical experience. She did not know that was what she was doing but nonetheless, she was able to do it almost at will and with very little effort. Doing so brought her great comfort and a physical sensation of calm elation.

In the last throes of Spring afternoons, she would lay down in the long grass where the fields roll up towards the hills, close her eyes and bask in the nourishing warmth of the falling sun. The trilling coos of woodpigeons were a beacon calling her away, a signal for her muscles to soften; a metronome, tuning in to the rise and fall of her rib cage.

Soon enough the glow would arrive.

And though B was there, present in that moment and that place, she was also not there. Or rather, she was everywhere. She was in the breeze that brushed her skin. She was in the leaves that rustled in the far-off trees and in the rays of light that kissed her brow. She was the beating heart of the wood pigeon and the blades of grass on which she lay. She was the sun and the cloudless sky. Her body had seemingly shut down and yet her senses werc acutely attuned to every change and shift around her.

She might remain in this state for a matter of minutes but for B it felt as though she had been away for both a few seconds and for many years. Time had not stood still; it was more like time had run sideways and B was stepping in and over and through it.

During late Spring and all the way through to early Autumn, B was able to achieve this altered state whenever she chose simply by curling up in the long grass, tuning in to the sounds around her and lazing in the nuzzling glow of the sun. The light and the warmth of the sun seemed to be the only true pre-requisite.

By late Autumn, when the sun was lower in the sky and the days became cooler, B found that she was no longer able to 'journey' as she called it. Nevertheless, at around the age of seven or eight, B found that she was able to wake in her own dreams and to control them. She would run freely through the grass fields and at her choosing would fly up, up over the hills and soar high into the brilliant blue sky. Like Icarus without the worry of wax, she would circle upwards on thermals, soaring higher and higher in the life-giving heat of the sun.

By the time B reached the age of eleven or twelve, she was no longer able to achieve any kind of altered state – neither through deep relaxation nor through lucid dreaming. As is the way, the child grew up. Too much happened to her. Too much happened around her. She continued to try but to no avail. She could never empty herself or clam her mind sufficiently. She could no longer attune with the rhythm of the swaying grass. The coo of the wood pigeons and the steady beat of her heart, once such familiar friends, became strangers. The heat of the sun never again felt so warm. And so, the deep, blissful elation she had become so accustomed to, slowly withered away to a faint memory before finally being entirely extinguished.

OPPORTUNITIES

(Things you might do for yourself)

- Sit, settle and listen. Go and sit in the sun. Go and sit on the grass or under a tree. Go with no intention and with no motivation other than to settle and listen. Take only yourself. Leave all other distractions behind. Settle yourself. Settle your breath. Listen to the sounds. Attune to your surroundings. Simply be.

AFFIRMATIONS

(Things you might say to yourself)

- I am in nature and nature is in me. We are one and the same.

- The child's mind and heart are open to all possibilities. Like a child, I am open to all possibilities.

SELF REFLECTION

(Things you might ask yourself)

- How much of the world around you are you no longer attuned to? How much of the world do you intentionally block out?

- How often do you make time for yourself? Just you, without distractions and without the clamour of other people?

- What is the current state of your dreams? And how often do you take time to reflect upon them?

2 LOST

By the time she was in her late teens, B was utterly lost.

Her family had dragged themselves through shared trauma, redundancy, and devastating episodes of poor mental health. Her parents had separated, and her elder brother had long since left.

B scraped through school and left with passable qualifications. Anxiety drained her of her zest and fear stripped her of desire. She was left with the aching knowledge that she had not fulfilled her potential and that she had not been happy for a long, long time.

B filled the void of all she might've been with shame and anger – two of the most potently destructive emotions anyone can experience. She was full to the brim of anguish and pain and yet she felt entirely empty of anything. She was devoid of purpose or direction. She did not feel as though there was anyone she could turn to for help and she did not know what to do. Above all, she felt disconnected – disconnected from everything and everyone, not least herself.

I imagine that many of you reading this will have felt like that at some point in your life. Perhaps you are feeling that way right now? Perhaps you have been running on empty for a sustained period so that you're burnt out emotionally and physically. Perhaps you've lived day after day, month after month unchallenged, unfulfilled, and unwell. If so, you will understand exactly how B was feeling. She was existing but she was not living.

In response to her existence, B had a very natural and very common reaction – she simply wanted to escape and to escape on a grand scale. Now, be sure to realise that to escape is not the same as running away. To escape is to thrive whereas running away is to survive. To escape is to acknowledge all that you might be whereas running away is to deny it. To escape is a leap forwards to freedom. To escape is a choice, a choice of a better life in which you feel purposeful and fulfilled.

B's intuition told her that her escape was to be found across the ocean, deep in the vast forests of the Americas.

Once, during a sleepover with a girl friend who had travelled through India and Nepal, B listened to the grounding hum of the meditation bowl. That night, she dreamed she was a bird flying through the canopy of a dense, verdant forest. Below her she saw a group of people walking through the forest floor. And in the next moment she was one of the people looking up at the bird as it swooped over them. The bird was leading the group through the forest. In the morning, B told her friend about the dream. In reply, her friend told her very plainly and quite seriously that the bird was B's spirit guide and that it would lead her to an important discovery. B believed it to be true, though she was unsure why.

In the forest, that is where B would find and be found.

OPPORTUNITIES
(Things you might do for yourself)

- Micro-escape. At some point we will all experience that feeling of being trapped – a feeling that is very often fuelled by our own anxieties and fears. When you start to feel that way, it is time to make an escape. And remember, not all escapes need to be on a grand scale! When you feel that dreaded emptiness closing in on you, seek out green spaces, vistas, running water or wildlife. Allow nature to be your support mechanism. Just 20 minutes in a natural setting can be all you need to reset and assist you in self-regulating. Acknowledge and escape. Ensure that you follow through on the advice that you would readily give to others - look after yourself (truly).

AFFIRMATIONS
(Things you might say to yourself)

- I am not defined by my past. I am not defined by my current situation.

- I give myself permission to escape. I give myself permission to free myself from everyone and everything.

- *My* future is derived from *my* actions and *my* choices. I define myself.

SELF REFLECTION
(Things you might ask yourself)

- What is it that is making you feel trapped? Sometimes

it is ourselves. Sometimes it is our situation. It might be your job, your relationships, or a general lack of fulfilment. Have you acknowledged your needs and your wishes? Have you communicated your hopes and ambitions?

- Many of us feel a sense of emptiness and experience a lack of purpose. It is important to ask yourself what is preventing you from making your escape? What have you got to lose or gain from taking a leap towards your freedom?

- Intuition is a powerful guide. How often do you listen to your gut? Trust yourself to know what is best for you.

3 ACTION

B had listened to her intuition, and she was now fully aware that her path was leading to the forests of Latin America. Where she would go, what she would do and who she would meet were details that were yet to be decided or discovered. One thing she was certain of however, was that she would need a significant sum of money to get there – money she didn't presently have.

B was a grafter and had never shirked hard work. Something drew her to night work. Not least the fact that night shifts tended to pay better. B gained employment working in the bakery of large supermarket and she very quickly discovered that working night shifts attracts a certain sort of person. Some, like her, were lost and broken. Some were desperate and some were unstable. Most were lonely and most were scared. But all of them, without exception, were hiding. They were hiding from the daylight, from the glaring light of reality.

The other thing B soon discovered about the night shifters is that many of her colleagues were self-medicating. Be it drink, drugs, prescription medicines or a combination of all three, many of them felt the need to dull the acute sharpness of their pain. In short, they were blunting the reality of their lived experience. Just taking the edge off. Just enough to get by. It wasn't at all unusual for the bakers to turn up drunk having come to work straight from the pub or for someone to take a line or pop a pill midway through the shift in the dead hours of the night. B thought it miraculous that as a team they ever produced anything remotely edible. As it happened, the products and in particular, the loaves of bread were always baked with deep care and precision.

Despite, (or perhaps, because of) all their frailties, B felt wholly at ease among her colleagues in the bakery. Likewise, they all immediately took B under their collective wing and soon enough counted her as one of their own. She was humble, kind and fiercely intelligent - for these reasons she was universally respected and held in high esteem. Whenever there was a question to be answered or a point to be settled, it was always to B that they turned to as the ultimate arbiter.

As the weeks and months of working through the night passed by, B's bank account gradually grew but her mood steadily declined. Sleeping through the day and then working for hours and hours under the he stark, soulless glare of the white strip lights was squeezing the life right out of her. Incessantly, those lights pushed down on her, creating a claustrophobia of the spirit. Every night there'd be a moment when she'd stop and stare right back up at those lights and silently curse them.

During her breaks in the beige cafeteria, sipping lukewarm tea, she would focus her gaze on the garish plastic plants in the corners; lifeless and dust-covered they served no purpose other than to highlight their own artificiality and painfully point out the total lack of natural light anywhere in the building. Plastic. Lifeless. Collecting dust.

In the warehouse behind the bakery, B would watch in amazement as pallet after pallet of fresh products from all around the world were delivered, unpacked and distributed to the shelves. It was endless. Always pristine and always wrapped in shimmering plastic.

At the sight of this relentless train of food, B would imagine herself zooming upwards out of the ceiling and up above the supermarket, and then up higher still until she could see all the supermarkets in the town and higher until she could see the lights of all the surrounding towns. And she would be struck by the realization that she worked in just one small supermarket in one small town among thousands. And the higher she went, the more she could fathom the true scale of the national and global network of food and plastic. Constant and colossal. She could see the food miles ticking up, the churning engines polluting 24/7, the mountains of plastic debris, the boundless whirring of electric meters and machines. Mass production had become mass destruction.

B knew she was part of the problem. She was a mass consumer. She worked at the supermarket. She ate the food. She relied on the corporate machine of mass production as heavily as anyone. She absolutely understood that she was contributing to the issues, but she felt helpless. She didn't know what to do, but she knew that she had to do something. This was her time to act.

B had saved some money. It wasn't much but it was probably enough to get her to her forest. And so as soon as she could, she handed in her notice. As she walked out of the supermarket after her last night shift, B stared up at those stark, artificial lights one more time and bade them a silent farewell. She stepped out into the joyous freshness of a Spring morning - her face warmed by the life-giving, life-affirming, wholly natural light of our sun.

OPPORTUNITIES
(Things you might do for yourself)

- Perspective is important but action is vital. Even in our darkest times, knowing where we are and being able to see where we are going is fundamental to our self-fulfilment. However, nothing changes without action. Acknowledge where you are now – be honest and be clear – state where you are going and then take action to get there. Massive, sustained action is the key to bringing about change in your life. Now is your time.

AFFIRMATIONS
(Things you might say to yourself)

- To change my life, I must change what I do. There is no change without action.
- I see the truth of my own situation and know that I can change it.
- Everything is temporary. Change is natural and necessary.

SELF REFLECTION
(Things you might ask yourself)

- To what extent are you hiding from the light of your own reality?
- Thinking about your own daily experience, to what extent are you self-medicating? In what way is this helping or hindering you?

- Look around you. How much of what we surround ourselves is artificial? How much of what we consume serves no purpose?

4 GUIDE

Before the internet made everything instantly searchable, we relied on books, maps, word of mouth, generational knowledge, and chance to inform our life choices. And so it was when B found her forest. She had been rooting around in the basement of vast second-hand bookshop – a place she had been many times before and that smelt of damp and forgotten lives. It was there that B stumbled on a guidebook that listed hundreds of opportunities all over the world offering people the chance to volunteer on social or ecological projects or to do some good working with charities.

> 'Volunteers required to help preserve 25 hectares of virgin cloud forest in the heart of the Talamanca mountains in Costa Rica. Must be physically fit, willing and conscientious. Send a letter of application to Lina de Pela at the Althea Cloud Forest Preserve …'

As soon as B read the words, she knew that this was the place. There were hundreds of similar listings and opportunities, but this was the one. B felt it. She felt it in her heart and deep in her gut.

B bought the book and with enormous excitement and a mounting sense of adventure, she wrote a long, heartfelt letter to Lina expressing her deep desire to come to the cloud forest. She posted the letter to Costa Rica and then waited. And she waited. And she waited. And while she waited, her every thought centred around that letter and the reply she so keenly sought. B ran through every possibility and outcome in her head a thousand times over: she had written the address incorrectly; the letter had never arrived; the letter had arrived, but Lina did not think she was good enough to go; and so on, and so on. B even considered the possibility that the cloud forest preserve did not even exist and that it was some sort of hoax or scam or a dream she had created.

When the reply did finally arrive, B held it in her hands as it if were an ancient artefact - something to be revered and treasured. She studied the envelope intently – the handwriting, the stamp, the crinkles – everything about it felt special, felt sacred to her. B opened it. Inside the envelope was a short, handwritten letter and on a separate sheet, there was a hand drawn map. B flicked her eyes across the map in absolute awestruck wonder and then she read the letter.

> 'Dear B,
>
> I know that you will soon be with us. Here, the forest floor has bathed in the glow of the moon 100,000 times before now but soon you will take your first steps among the magnificent trees – here we have white oaks and laurels. The forest is a magical place. You will discover that for yourself, I am sure. Each day, the clouds blow across the valley into the forest, and we are veiled in a cool, white mist. Here, you will find many species of plants and animals. You might spend a lifetime here

and still be surprised. This is a special place. Bring warm clothes – the nights are cold here. And a coat to keep you dry – we have lots of rain. Reading your letter, I know that your heart is full of goodness. I look forward to seeing your face, holding your hands in mine and welcoming you to our home

Yours,
Lina De Pela

B immediately read the short letter again and immediately she bestowed legendary status upon Lina. In Lina, B knew that she had found a poet, a seer, a guide, a kindred spirit and a woman of immense warmth and humble profundity. B smiled as she felt a wave of true happiness flow through her.

B turned her attention to the hand drawn map. It was a guide to reach the cloud forest from the main road. On the map, the track to the forest was a snaking path traversing across many rivers and streams. At the main road there was only one clue about where to head to – a hotel marked with an arrow and next to it a small note: 'Ask the bus driver to stop at the Hotel Jaco and walk from there.'

B clasped the letter and the map close to her chest and had a little cry to herself. For the first time in a long while, she knew where she was going.

OPPORTUNITIES

(Things you might do for yourself)

- Trust your gut and listen to your heart. Learn to tune into the insights that your own intuition is offering up. There is a reason that we return to some places repeatedly. Similarly, there are some people who we encounter that are keyholders – they will open the door to the next chapter in our lives. When these people enter our lives, we must recognize them and understand that we have a choice to step through that door. Listen to your heart. Trust your gut. Be brave. Step across that threshold.

AFFIRMATIONS

(Things you might say to yourself)

- I am not alone. There are many people who will support and guide me. I might not have met them yet, but I know that I will.

- Progress is happiness. When I am moving towards my goals, I am stepping into my own happiness.

SELF REFLECTION

(Things you might ask yourself)

- Are there places that you keep on returning to? What is drawing you back there? Is it a feeling? What is waiting to be discovered? What is it that the place offers you?

- Serendipity. Coincidence. Synchronicity. Thinking about a certain person and then you bump into them.

Have a feeling that something will happen and then it does. Whatever the reason, these things exist and occur. How might you tune into these moments? How might they benefit you? How might you influence this phenomenon?

5 CHANGE

The bus station in central San José made B realise that, even in her relatively short life, she has seen far too little of life and of the world. Here, it seemed to her, all life congregated and thronged. All noise, all grime, all scents, all colours, all emotions, and sentiment were being pulled to this point and were being amplified. This was life with the volume turned right up.

B was utterly entranced and totally overwhelmed. She felt entirely out of place. Fear and exhilaration coursed through her body in equal measure. She was a very, very long way from home and all she had to aid her were a pocket-guide to Costa Rica, the entirety of her savings exchanged into colones, a journal, some photos of her family, and of course, Lina's letter and the hand drawn map.

Through a combination of pure chance and perseverance B eventually manged to find the correct bus (among the hundreds there) that would take her south on the Pan-American highway into the Talamanca mountains. Her bus did not leave for another hour and so B took respite from the intense tropical heat and diesel fumes in the welcoming shade one of the many small, rickety cafes (or sodas as they are known in Costa Rica) that surrounded the bus station.

Inside the 'Soda Pina', B ordered the cheapest dish on the menu (arroz con pinto) and a café con leche. The waitress asked B where she was from and where she was going and took a genuine interest when B told her. As she was talking, B realised that the girl was probably about her age, possibly even a year or two younger. She was friendly and her smile spoke of sincerity and warmth – as was the way with so many of the Ticos that B encountered.

B sipped and ate and watched the world go by. The frenetic comings and goings of the buses and the passengers were captivating. At that moment, B was struck by her own smallness in the world. She was suddenly aware that all this was going on at the bus station every single day - all these people, all this energy and direction – all in perpetual movement and constant flux. And she was acutely aware that she was only witnessing a tiny glimpse; this was just one bus station among hundreds across Costa Rica, not to mention at home and of course, everywhere else across the globe. Similar scenes were being played out in thousands and thousands of towns and cities, twenty-four hours a day, seven days a week and this had been going on long before B arrived and would continue long after she left. The world was immense, and the world was moving, and B was one very, very tiny part of it.

For a fleeting moment, B felt something that she had not encountered since her childhood – it was a sense of reassurance and connection that was born from recognising that she was tiny and impermanent. She felt comforted by these insights, and as she stepped out of the soda, B noticed that the colours seemed a little brighter, the noises more distinct. Everything was clearer.

B found her bus, clambered aboard and in her broken Spanish asked the driver to stop at the Hotel Jaco, just as Lina's letter had instructed. The driver smiled, nodded, and said something B couldn't make out. B smiled, nodded, thanked him, and shuffled down the narrow aisle to her seat.

Looking around, it was clear to B that she was the only non-Tico passenger aboard. This was not a tourist bus. In fact, the interior of the bus seemed to be a cliché of itself – every available inch was crammed with people, packages, goods, bags, blankets, machine parts and of course, the obligatory chickens. This is what she came for, she told herself. And as she settled in for the journey ahead, she gazed out of the dusty windows and welcomed the warmth of the tropical sun on her face.

The road and traffic were like nothing she had ever experienced. The drivers seemed to be a law unto themselves; willing participants in some sort of non-sanctioned, cross-country race where overtaking at any cost and the prolific honking of horns were standard practices to be savoured and undertaken at every opportunity.

The road often narrowed as it circumvented colossal mountain spurs and buses passed within inches of each other. At the apex of these hairpin turns, B gazed down at the 1000ft sheer drop below her window, her fists gripped in fear. She looked around the bus for signs of reassurance or mutual concern from her fellow passengers – none of whom seem remotely bothered by the prospect of certain death that was less that tyre's width away. At certain points, landslides, thick with mud and rock, had spilled out onto the road meaning only a single lane served all the traffic. Here, rather than waiting to pass safely, traffic from both directions squeezed passed each other in the one lane. Again, B thought the risky manoeuvre was highly dangerous but everyone else on the bus seemed utterly oblivious.

Whenever the bus stopped or slowed, a gaggle of young children would leap aboard. They carried armfuls of nuts, fruits, chips, or other snacks that they would sell for a few colones. B simply shook her head at the many offers and watched mesmerised as, at a holler from the driver, the children would scramble off the bus, run alongside as it began to pull away and then climb onto the back of the bus, clinging on for their lives until the next stop or landslide or station allowed them to board another ride. At first, B thought they were mad, but she soon realised that their risk-taking was born out of necessity; these children were scraping a meagre living from the road. Poverty was all around her. It was in the faces of those children, in the hard-skinned hands of the workers on the bus, in the clothes, and in the make do and mend machinery she saw everywhere. From that point on, she always purchased a small bag of the offered goods – a few colones to her was nothing, but to these children it was a step closer to survival.

Every day since she arrived in Costa Rica, the rain had arrived mid-afternoon like clockwork. It poured coolness and life over the sweltering land. On cue, huge drops galloped against the bus window and the drumming stirred B from the slumber she'd fallen into. The terrain had changed since B last looked out, now the road was lined by vast trees. This was forest.

A short time later, the bus slowed to a halt. The driver turned to look back over his shoulder and called out 'Hotel Jaco'. For some reason it did not register with B. The driver turned back, looked directly at B in the large mirror above his head and pointing to the roadside he called again, 'This is Hotel Jaco.'

B shot up like a bolt, grabbed her bag, bumped her way down the aisle, hurriedly thanked the driver and disembarked onto the side of the road. The bus pulled away, drove around the next bend and was out of sight in seconds.

B stood entirely still for a moment or two. She suddenly felt very alone and very vulnerable. Then she reached down into her pocket and pulled out the hand drawn map that Lina had sent her. Unfolding it, she whispered to herself, 'Nearly there now, nearly there.' And she set off down the road.

OPPORTUNITIES

(Things you might do for yourself)

- Seek out the extraordinary. What is normal for one person is wholly unusual or exotic for another. Recognise that we all have a comfort zone that we tend to gravitate towards. Identify yours and then make a conscious effort to break out of it. Go somewhere new, take a different route, do something different, try that activity you've always considered. Explore. Be bold. Stepping into the unknown, breaking out of your comfort zone and discovering the extraordinary in life will light a fire in you. Transformation will follow.

AFFIRMATIONS

(Things you might say to yourself)

- I am tiny. I am temporary.

- Everything I do has meaning and significance, and it is me alone that gives it meaning and significance. My experience is valid.

- I am grateful for all that I have.

- I am exploring. I am seeking out new experiences. The path I tread is mine alone to decide.

SELF REFLECTION

(Things you might ask yourself)

- How much exhilaration is there in your life? When you consider your daily routine what words spring to mind? Monotonous? Mundane? Unfulfilling? What are the barriers that are preventing you from changing that? Are the barriers insurmountable? Are the barriers self-imposed? Is it possible that the fear of what *might* happen is holding you back from breaking free? Why is the certainty and security of the ordinary and the known, however mundane, more appealing than the risk of freedom and fulfilment? In short, what have you got to lose?

6 DESCENT

Without too much trouble, B found the dirt track that led off the main road. She stepped off the road, onto the orange dust of the track and took a moment to consult her map. She was heading down into a valley. Scanning the vista, she could see a scattering of homes and huts far away on the opposite slope of the valley – that was the small village that she was heading towards. Lina's forest was near there.

Looking at the distance she had to cover and the gradient of the hillside, B felt a pang of uncertainty and apprehension wash over her whole body. She looked again at the hand drawn map which now seemed woefully sparse and lacking in detail compared to the web of tracks and streams and bridges she could see in the valley below her. In one corner of the map was written an instruction: 'Always keep right.' B imagined that this was in case of passing vehicles – in the same way she would face oncoming traffic when walking down the country lanes back home. B gathered herself. She had her map, she took a sip of water and set off resolutely down the track, estimating that it would take her an hour of solid walking to reach the homes on the other side of the valley.

Within a few steps, the far-reaching, expansive vistas of

the valley were hidden by the thick vegetation and towering trees that closed in on either side of the narrow track. B's gaze though was fixed firmly on the track ahead of her; every step was a potential pitfall - loose rocks, divots and protruding boulders punctuated the pot-holed surface. Every step was precarious; the uneven track cambered to the side and undulated this way and that. Even though she was heading downwards towards the main river at the valley floor, B found herself climbing up and down constantly as the track twisted and turned over the terrain. B slipped and skidded many times and soon the heels of her hands and her knuckles were grazed and pocked with blood. Sweat soaked her body and clothes, so much so that each time she stumbled and fell, the dust stuck to her, coating her in a layer of earthy, orange grime.

Descending further and further the temperature cooled. The vegetation became even more dense and even more verdant. Her ears pulsed with blood flow, and this was mirrored by the gushing of rapidly flowing water – the river was getting nearer.

The track continued to twist down the valley, like a vine wrapping itself around the thick trunk of a tree. One more horse-shoe bend brought B face to face with the river. The track disappeared into the water. It was a shallow enough crossing for a 4x4 vehicle or for confident horses, but B could see that the rushing water meant that this was no place to be crossing on foot. With some degree of panic, B consulted her map; to her relief, a bridge was marked a little way off. B followed the river upstream and sure enough she soon came to a rickety mishmash of timber, wire and rope that might once possibly have passed as a bridge but now, to B's eyes, looked even more of a death-trap than the fast-flowing white water below it.

'You haven't come this far to give up now,' she reminded herself as she grasped the rope handrail and pulled herself onto the bridge. Very tentatively and using every ounce of her dexterity and determination she pulled herself across the bridge. All the while, the water below ran fast and free over huge, smooth boulders.

For a moment, B was outside of herself and could see herself on the bridge. Her wariness and the stiffness of her body were magnified. She could see how awkwardly she groped and how much she strained, and she could not help laughing at herself. Here, in this incredible valley she was as separate from nature as she could possibly be.

With a heavy, clumsy thud B jumped down from the bridge onto the riverbank. She had made it. But B's triumph was short-lived, the descent to the river was only the beginning of her journey to the forest.

OPPORTUNITIES

(Things you might do for yourself)

- Part and apart. We are very much a part of nature even though it so often feels that we are apart from it. Getting off the beaten track and immersing ourselves in the natural world provides the opportunity for us to reflect on how distant the separation might've become and how far we might have travelled away from our connection with Mother Earth.

AFFIRMATIONS

(Things you might say to yourself)

- I slip and I stumble because I am human.
- When the way is blocked, I do not give up.
- Sometimes moving sideways allows me to move forwards.

SELF REFLECTION

(Things you might ask yourself)

- When the world closes in around us and we are alone, the singular thing that always remains is choice. We can choose to relent. We can choose to turn back. We can choose to move forwards. What choices will you make in the days and months ahead? How might your choices be creating unnecessary barriers and blocking you from your goal? How will your choices help you discover and explore?

7 FOUND

Soaked through with sweat and covered head to toe in a thin film of dirt, B felt shaky, tired and increasingly overwhelmed by the daunting climb ahead. As she set out on the track once more, she immediately noticed the strain the steep incline put on her calves and feet. The unsteady surface required careful navigation. Her breathing began to get heavier. Her backpack pulled on her shoulders and dug into her back. Her head began to throb.

On the descent there had only been a single track to follow. Now as she climbed upwards, the track forked off in many directions. All around her she could see homesteads sparsely dotted about the hillside. At each fork in the track B consulted her map and though it was clearly not to scale or particularly detailed, B felt confident she was heading in the right direction. All the while, she always stayed on the right-hand side of the track, just as the instructions on the map advised. That said, B hadn't encountered a single vehicle and as such, this warning was so far unnecessary.

Head down, B drove onwards and upwards, planting one foot in front of the other. It was now late in the afternoon and her shadow stretched out further and further ahead of her on the dusty track. The intense heat of the early afternoon was quickly giving way to chilly coolness.

As B climbed, the steady, rhythmic plodding of her feet hypnotised her and her thoughts flew far away from that hillside in Costa Rica. She remembered people and events from the past that she had long forgotten. She was transported back to being a very young girl, walking with her mother and father either side of her, holding her hands. She remembered giggling with delight as they swept her up and swung her forwards. That laugh, that joy, that sense of security and warmth were precious memories that she had nearly lost forever.

Back in the present, back on the hillside, B was crying big tears that rolled over the dirt and dust on her cheeks and dripped off her chin. B wiped them away and continued to climb higher and higher.

The map was no longer consulted. It stayed crumpled in the clammy and dusty grip of her clenched fist. Even when she tripped forward in the fading light her hand did not open to stop her fall, instead it continued to grasp the languishing map so that her knuckles crashed against the rocky ground and tore her dry skin. Now as she walked, blood trickled over and around the contours of her hand and dropped to the floor so that bright red drops rained down onto the orange-ochre dust and left a trail of blood, like breadcrumbs marking her path.

And on she climbed. In a trance. In a state of delirium. Step after step. Plodding on. Ploughing on. Higher up the hillside. The track turned to path; path turned to scrub. Day turned to night. Hillside became mountain slope. Exhausted and cold B came to a stop. Her feet throbbed and so did her head. She looked at her bloodied hand and then in the cool evening air she woke from her trance.

All at once B realised, she was lost. Then the gravity of her situation crept up on her – she had no means of contacting Lina, or anyone else for that matter. She knew then that if she did not find shelter or help soon, there was a very real risk of her becoming unwell through exposure or dehydration.

For the first time since she had started the ascent from the river below, B turned to face the valley she had climbed. She had enough presence of mind to know that her best chance of survival was to retrace her steps back down the slope and find one of the isolated homesteads she had spotted earlier. Without any further hesitation she set off again back down the mountainside. Down and down until the track started to fork off into different trails. She picked a fork and followed it. Sure enough, it led to a small home – now just a shadow in the dusk.

The elderly man who answered the door had quite a shock. This was not the sort of place one had visitors simply dropping by. Moreover, B was a shivering, bloodied mess and could barely talk. She could only manage to say Lina's full name which she repeated several times. She could not recall any of her rudimentary Spanish and the gentlemen spoke no English. B repeated Lina's name once more and without consciously doing so, raised her fist and brandished the crumpled map level with the man's confounded face.

Very carefully, he unfurled B's fingers and took the map. Instantly, the man understood the situation. Pointing on the map he spoke very quickly and very assuredly, nodding and glancing at B the whole time. B stood perfectly still. She did not understand anything he had said. The man darted back into his house and returned a few moments later holding a large glass of cool, still lemonade and a red pen. He put the drink in B's hand and she gulched it down in a few swallows. On the map, the man drew a thick red line that indicated the path for B to follow to Lina's cloud forest.

'Gracias,' B croaked as she handed the chilled glass back to the man. He took the glass and with his round, sturdy index finger he traced B's route on the map and then traced it again pointing out across the slope.

'Mucho gusto. Mucho gusto,' B gushed, coming to her senses a little.

'Mucho gusto!' the elderly gentleman replied and smiled

broadly as he gave B a little wave of his hand as she set off.

By the time she reached the cloud forest it was past midnight. The final part of her trek had been lit by moonlight. She had arrived under the gaze of the Milky Way. All space and time had brought to this moment. Safely and mostly intact, she had arrived at her destiny.

The clinging, sweet aroma of a Costa Rican cigar filled B's nostrils; powerful and leathery, it was a scent B would never forget. There on the porch, sat Lina's husband Higuel. A bright red baseball cap and a thick white beard framed a face that sang of experience and eyes that whispered of suffering. A bear of a man in his late seventies, Higuel had fled a life of oppression to seek out a life of spiritual and artistic freedom; he was a painter, a poet, and a pioneer in all that he did.

Without saying a word, Higuel took B's hand in his paw and shook it. That handshake said: 'Yes! You made it!' and also, 'Thank God you're safe!' and also, 'At last I can go to bed!'

Higuel took B's backpack and led her up to the small cabin that would be her home for the foreseeable future. As they set off, the young Alsatian that had been sitting adoringly beside Higuel scrambled to its feet and walked patiently at his side.

The cabin was very simply constructed and very sparsely furnished. There was a bed, a lamp, a single window, and separate toilet. Higuel laid the backpack down beside the bed and with a touch of his cap he left.

Eyes wide open, B collapsed backwards onto the bed and basked in the moonlight that flooded through the window. She was numb.

Moments later, B could hear Higuel's heavy gait on the wooden steps leading up to the cabin accompanied by the light patter of paws. Higuel knocked on the door and B pulled her aching body off the bed to answer. With a nod and a smile, Higuel handed her a small, round tray on which lay a plate of warm empanadas, a mug of hot chocolate and a carafe of chilled water. Higuel wished her good night, and both he and his shadow left once again.

B drank and ate and collapsed. As her eyes closed, she felt elation and relief that she had made it. By hook or by crook she had arrived.

OPPORTUNITIES

(Things you might do for yourself)

- The importance of adversity. A life without challenges is no life at all. Many people's idea of the perfect life equates to the easy life. But without challenge and sacrifice there is little sense of reward or fulfilment. Once you discover your goal you must pursue it relentlessly. Yes, it will be hard. Yes, there will be times when you will want to quit. But you will meet the challenges and in doing so, you will meet your true self.

AFFIRMATIONS

(Things you might say to yourself)

- I am strong. I am capable. I achieve.

- I am independent but I am always open to help and guidance from others.

SELF REFLECTION

(Things you might ask yourself)

- The path we take is full of wrong turns and missteps. There are many times that we stray from the track and get lost. How might you react the next time you lose direction? How willing might you be to accept the help of others?

- Why is it important for you to pursue your goals and realise your vision? What is the purpose that sits behind your drive? By all means, make a list of your goals but before you set out to accomplish them, it is imperative that you fully work out and articulate the 'why'. Why is this important to you? Why does this matter so much? Why will this change your life or that of your family? The 'why' will keep you driving up that mountain when all else has failed.

8 RELEASE

What felt like just a few minutes later, Higuel was once again knocking gently on the weathered wood of the cabin door. 'Buenos días. You slept a long time.'

Now, instead of moonlight, it was the light of the sun that poured into the small room. At some point in the night B had been awoken by the chattering of her own teeth. It had become incredibly cold, and she had climbed gratefully into her sleeping bag still fully clothed. Now, she was overly warm, and her skin was clammy with sweat. She wrestled herself out of the bag, got herself washed, dressed as quickly as she could and trotted the short distance across to the main cabin.

'Hola pura vida!' Lina welcomed B with a broad smile and then a long, tight hug during which Lina hummed reassuringly through closed lips. It was a distinctly maternal embrace – protective, reassuring, and loving. For a moment, everything stopped; B felt calm and peaceful. Before B could even utter a word, Lina was off and away busying herself with preparing breakfast.

Lina was older than B had imagined – B guessed she was in her mid to late sixties. A short, strong woman whose eyes were dark and brimming with wisdom and tragedy. Her hands were worker's hands, her skin polished by the elements. Everything about Lina radiated integrity and pragmatism.

To B's relief, Lina spoke good English and as she prepared the scrambled eggs and hot, strong coffee she bombarded B with question after question about her journey, her family, and her life back home. The confusion over Lina's hand drawn map was soon cleared up – 'Always keep right' had meant always take the right turn and not, as B had imagined, keep on the right-hand side of the road. Lina apologised profusely but B reassured her that the fault lay with her and not with Lina.

B talked more to Lina over that breakfast than she had to anybody else for some time. In particular, she was not used to talking about herself, but in doing so with Lina, she felt a sense of relief and acceptance.

The creaking of the wooden cabin, the welcoming aroma of freshly brewed coffee and the melodic tone of Lina's voice all resonated deeply within B and gave her comfort and security.

After breakfast, B washed and dried the plates and pots, and then put everything away in the correct place according to Lina's instructions. When it was done Lina said, 'Vámonos. I will show you the forest,' and they set off together, B following in Lina's footsteps.

Immediately, B was in awe. The forest was, just as Lina said, 'Still as God had made it' – virgin, primary cloud forest, thousands of years old. Every possible space was blooming in an unbridled abundance of nature. The many hues of black and brown on the forest floor gave rise to all possible shades of green. Verdant. Wet. Still. Startling.

Lina toured B around the dedicated walking trails that she had mapped out and created over the years. At every step, she pointed out the flora and fauna that surrounded them: the giant white oaks; the gnarled laurels; the bromeliads; the lichens; the beetles. And though they didn't see one, Lina was most excited when telling B about the animal that best represented the grace and mystery of the cloud forest – the Resplendent Quetzal. Lina shared her detailed knowledge of the seemingly sacred bird and described its stunning green and red plumage and its spiritual significance to the Mayan people, to whom it was a symbol of light and good.

'If you are lucky enough to see a quetzal then you are truly blessed,' said Lina.

They walked and walked. At certain points, Lina stopped to give B some direction on what might be done to maintain the existing trails. The preserve was over 25 hectares and yet Lina seemed to know every turn and every individual tree. Where B slipped and tripped, Lina's every step was sure and steady.

Lina led them to the edge of the forest, where they looked out over the valley that B had descended and climbed the day before.

'We are at 8.500 feet altitude,' Lina explained. 'Here, you can walk in the clouds.' And so it was. As they peered out over the valley, great swatches of brilliant white cloud blew towards them. Seconds later a swathe of the cloud surrounded them so that they were shrouded in a cloak of barely penetrable mist. B laughed out loud and turned to Lina with a huge smile.

'Yes, I know! It is very beautiful,' said Lina. 'Now B, you are a cloud walker!'

The clouds drifted into the forest and the pair followed them. As they wound their way back into the depths of the forest, Lina reminded B to look up: 'There is so much to see in front of you that you forget to look up!' And of course, she was right. B stopped and tracked the trajectory of the enormous tree trunks up and up to the canopy above. There, the sunlight broke through the canopy in streams of light. Again, the sight made B grin from ear-to-ear and once again she looked to Lina as if they were both sharing this experience for the very first time, but Lina was already a way off down the trail.

'Vamos!' she said, 'I have something I want you to do.'

As they walked together, Lina explained that the existing trails had been designed by Lina and created with the help of the many visitors to the preserve over the course of the past couple of decades. There were three trails: the main trail that circumnavigated the preserve was known as the yellow trail; the blue trail was a direct route from the cabins across to the many streams that criss-crossed the far side of the preserve: and finally, there was the red trail that took you to the vantage point with the spectacular views across the valley where they had just come from. At different points the three trails intersected and there were numerous other mini trails that connected them.

'I have been waiting for you to come here B," said Lina.

'Waiting? For me?' asked B, unsure what Lina meant.

'Yes. You will find the path for a new trail in the preserve. You will build the purple trail.'

B was speechless. She didn't know what to say and she didn't know why Lina would entrust her with such an important task. Sensing this, Lina continued, 'I have been waiting for the right person. Someone with the right spirit. You are that person. I know it.'

'Thank you,' was all that B could think to say.

'But not yet. First, you must know the forest. Vamos.' And with that, they walked back to the cabin, made lunch together and talked.

Over the next few days, B did very little in the forest except sit and think and listen. A cloud forest is not a noisy place. It is not the cacophony you might experience in a tropical rainforest. A cloud forest is mostly silent and for days B just listened. At first, the voice in her own head was overwhelming. B had always been aware of the near constant narration of her inner monologue but now, in this powerful, all-pervading silence she heard it truly for the first time; it was incessant, loud, and incredibly annoying.

For the first week or so in the forest, B felt exhausted and lethargic. She was not the least bit motivated to begin work on the new trail. Rather, she felt empty and whatever was left in her was still draining out – soaked up by the dense moss that grew voraciously everywhere that it could get a foothold.

And so it was, that B let herself be freed to the forest. She released herself. Her angst, her anxiety, her fears, her thoughts, her hopes, her desires, her past, her voice all began to be released to the mosses, to the earth, to the leaf litter, to the clouds. She bathed in the silence and the forest washed her.

OPPORTUNITIES

(Things you might do for yourself)

- The importance of letting go. We all have things we need to let go of. We all tend to hang on to ideas, memories and feelings that no longer benefit us. Likewise, we all experience times when we feel overwhelmed and overcome - we are full to the brim and cannot take any more. When we feel like this, aspects of our life tend to spill over and negatively impact our emotional, psychological, and physical wellbeing. At the point that we begin to feel overcome, it is essential to recognise that we need to release. Often the simplest and most impactful means of release is to immerse ourselves in the sounds and silences of the natural world. Find the space. Be in the space. Be silent. Listen. Release.

AFFIRMATIONS

(Things you might say to yourself)

- I am surrounded by life. I immerse myself in life and it sustains me.

- Life springs from death. Death is inevitable. I am part of this cycle. My life is now. My time is now.

SELF REFLECTION

(Things you might ask yourself)

- How much time do we spend looking down at the ground because we are afraid that we might trip? What are we missing out on by not looking up? For many of us, the fear of failure simply cements our own deep-felt insecurities. Is it time for you to stop looking down, to stop fearing the fall and to look up and look forward?

9 REPAIR

It took around three weeks for B to fully release. Three weeks of fatigue and lethargy. Three weeks of silence and acceptance. The voice in her head quietened to the point that the constant narration of negative self-talk and intrusive thoughts subsided almost entirely.

After that period, B reached a point when she was no longer tuned into herself but was tuned into the forest. Day after day she walked among the colossal tress of the virgin cloud forest. She was completely alone and completely free; free to explore and free to discover.

B's gaze had turned outwards, and she began to take notice of the wonders of the forest in far more detail and depth than she had done so far. In doing so, her senses seemed to bloom and flourish in response.

B began to examine the incredible structures and patterns of the trees and plants. She was fascinated by the regal splendour of the bromeliads that nestled thirty, forty feet up in the nook of a tree trunk. Their leaves arched open like grateful hands catching the life-giving rainwater that fell from above.

And B would trace her fingers down the notched and gnarled rivulets that formed the thick bark of the ancient trees. Every ridge and turn detected by her fingertips would send a surge of signals to her brain, firing connections, inspiring discovery and wonder.

The greens of the forest glowed in more hues than B thought possible. Each one made itself known to her and the more she took in, the more nuanced and subtle her appreciation and perception became.

The silence of the forest held her and comforted her. So much so, that B began to talk to the forest. She asked the forest questions in the same way that Lina had asked her all those questions when she had first arrived. What do you do? Where did you come from? Where are you going? What's your purpose? How do you connect to this and to that? Soon enough, the forest began to answer and to reveal itself to B. B learned that everything in the forest had a purpose and that nothing was superfluous or irrelevant. She learned that despite the thousands of different motivations, aims, needs, and drives at work within the forest, everything worked in serene harmony. The forest was a perfected system of giving, taking, sharing, recycling and renewal. The only thing that exerted its will over anything else was death. Death was the great certainty in the forest and death was the driving force of the cycle of harmony.

B dug her fingers into the rich, damp leaf mould, pulled a fistful of the decaying mass close to her nose and snuffed deeply. It was truly the scent of the Earth.

In the massive trunks of fallen trees, B observed the myriad of tunnels bored out by beetles and grubs. The process of the once solid tissue being transformed into a frail honeycomb and then eventually into powder was laid bare for her to see. Breaking down the old, giving rise to the new – that was the way of the forest.

One time, while clambering over the trunk of a fallen white oak, B unintentionally pulled away a large patch of bark. There, revealed in all its stark glory was an enormous, white grub, far bigger than any of B's fingers. B watched in total fascination as it fed on the decaying wood, breaking it down to build itself up; soon to metamorphosise into a magnificent beetle. With utmost care, B replaced the bark but that image of the grub, its glistening, pulsating, pearlescent body, was seared into her mind. Its energy, its work, and its determination were electrifying to B. In the many decades that passed after B left the cloud forest, she never forgot that grub. In that grub, in that moment, there B came to realise, was all the music of the universe. All solutions, all problems, all matters past, present and future, all philosophies, possibilities, and explanations could be found there. Death. Life. Recycling. Renewal. Repurposing. Transformation.

And sometime later, B recognised that she, of course, was that grub - chewing through the dead wood of her life, finding solace in the forest, driving forwards towards her own transformation until she too was ready to emerge.

OPPORTUNITIES

(Things you might do for yourself)

- Everyone, regardless of their age, role, lived experience, goals or beliefs, gets worn down by the daily challenges we face in our lives. We all need to give ourselves permission to repair. Set aside dedicated time, ideally every day but certainly every week as minimum, to find silence and solace in nature. Be sure to turn your inner gaze into an outer gaze. Become receptive to the wonders around you and to recognise your place and purpose in all things.

AFFIRMATIONS

(Things you might say to yourself)

- All solutions are found in me. I am capable. I am transforming.

- Looking outwards, I see myself. Seeing myself, I see all things.

SELF REFLECTION

(Things you might ask yourself)

- Harmony is nature's great accomplishment and its greatest gift. How might you find comfort and contentment within that harmony? What is your note in the music of the universe?

10 REFRESH

B soon became a child of the forest. The trails, streams, slopes and fallen trunks were her playground. She was more joyous and more energised than she could ever remember. She threw herself into divining the path for the new trail and spent hours and hours plotting, grafting, walking, clearing and creating, only returning to the cabin at dusk when the lack of light penetrating down to the forest floor made work impossible.

During the evenings, B and Lina deepened the strength of their bond. They would talk for hours about the forest, discussing specific trees or a particular point on a trail. They would eat simple foods - eggs, rice, tortillas, and fruit were the staples. Strong coffee or cloud forest water were the drinks of choice. Talk. Eat. Read. Walk. Work. Sleep.

Around this time, Lina's eldest son arrived at the forest. A wild, bright, brash young man, Andrés had been raised on the mean streets of Brooklyn and on the soft sands of the Dominican Republic. He was a walking compendium of comical stories and counterculture. He had been broken and had rebuilt himself. He was fragile and yet, so strong. There was great sorrow in his eyes and deep love in his heart.

During his visit, Andrés spent all day in the forest with

B. Every day, he made B laugh and every day he helped her learn. He regaled B with tales of his misspent youth in Brooklyn and of the many scrapes and close calls he had survived. He was beautifully imperfect.

Andrés showed B parts of the forest she had never seen, not least the 'Blind Bridge' – a huge, white oak that had fallen many, many years ago across a deep ravine that ran along the far edge of the preserve.

As was his nature, Andrés gambolled across the fallen behemoth without a care in the world, talking and laughing and smiling the whole while. Once on the other side, he immediately turned and beckoned B across. 'Come on!' he called, 'It's not hard. Don't overthink it!'

The trunk was vast. B clambered up onto the thick stub that was embedded deep into the earth. Here, the fall to the ground was a meagre five or six feet but B still felt wary. She looked across the ravine to Andrés who now seemed far, far away. She was sure he was hollering encouragement to her, but she couldn't hear him; B's entire universe had shrunk down to a bubble a few feet wide surrounding her.

As B took her first few steps across the trunk, she could not prevent herself looking to her left and right and then peering down, down into the bottom of the ravine. Now she could see the reality of the situation. She was easily 30 or 40 feet above the stream and boulders beneath. B's legs began to shake uncontrollably. To fall here would mean a serious injury at the least and very possibly death. B knew that medical assistance was many hours away. Her mind began racing with anxiety and she dropped down to her hands and knees. She couldn't do it; she knew she couldn't do it. Her inner voice was telling her, screaming at her, that it wasn't possible.

The trunk, as wide as it was, was also damp with the ever-present moisture, and slippery due to the moss that covered every possible inch of the forest. B's heart thumped hard in her chest, booming out an SOS. Her fingertips clenched into the soft moss, and she bowed her head down so that it rested for a moment on the mighty tree. She closed her eyes and breathed in. She breathed in the calmness and solidity of the great oak. Her nostrils flared and her lungs filled as she inhaled the aroma of the ancient forest – the rich, grounding scent of life and decay. As she breathed the forest in, she also breathed in hope.

B opened her eyes, lifted her head, and looked across to Andrés who was once again beckoning to her to cross the bridge. Though she still felt certain that she could not do it, something inside was telling her that it was possible. It was possible.

Carefully getting to her feet, standing tall, B felt the bubble of her universe that had been so close, expand outwards. She was able to hear Andrés calling to her, encouraging her. She looked at him and she smiled. Then the smile turned into a laugh as she began to take her first cautious steps.

By the time she reached the midpoint of the bridge, at what was the highest point above the stream below, B was filled with elation. She paused, raised both arms up above her head and let out a whoop of pure joy. It was shout that said to the forest, to the world and most importantly, to herself, 'I can do it! It is possible!' Then Andrés joined in with the whooping, celebrating her accomplishment and her newfound belief. Both of them beamed and laughed as B confidently strode across the remainder of the bridge and jumped down to the ground.

That was another watershed moment for B. She had sensed herself changing ever since she arrived at the forest but in that moment, she could really feel it. The transformation was tangible, and it was exhilarating. The grub was metamorphosising.

Not too long after that, Andrés left the forest to continue his own adventures. And though she searched and searched, B was never able to find the Blind Bridge again.

OPPORTUNITIES

(Things you might do for yourself)

- Inevitably, we will all encounter some people in our lives who want tear us down or hold us back. The fault lies with them and not with us. Equally, there will be some people we meet who will build us up – selflessly and often unknowingly. They encourage us and guide us to find our own path without imposing themselves or their purpose upon us. They imbue us with confidence and belief. They encourage and motivate us to overcome the barriers that stand in our way. They support our dreams and our goals without question. When these people enter your life, embrace them and be grateful.

AFFIRMATIONS

(Things you might say to yourself)

- It is possible.
- It is possible.
- It is possible.

SELF REFLECTION

(Things you might ask yourself)

- Transience is a defining and recurring feature of our lived experience. Moments, connections, meetings, and relationships are impermanent. So often, opportunities in our lives occur just once, never to be rediscovered. Consider some of the key events and relationships in your own life. How might the course of your life have run differently if you had or had not taken certain opportunities? How would your outlook and actions differ if you knew that a meeting or moment was the one and only opportunity you had?

11 RETURN

During the daytime B toiled away creating the new trail. It was hard work but hugely rewarding.

By evening she was exhausted, but she felt deep calm and contentment.

Nights brought her dreams of extraordinary vividness. To her joy, B found that the power of lucid dreaming had returned to her. In her most common, recurring dream she found herself walking the round, green hills near her childhood home. She would be climbing a hill and at times it became so steep that she would have to clamber on her hands and knees for fear of tumbling back down to the bottom. When she had reached the top, B would stand tall and seeing the green expanse reach out in every direction around her, she would stretch her arms above her head and then out to the sides. Then B would take a few steps back down the hill, steady at first so that she was just trotting, and then she would speed up, speed up, speed up so that she was running, running so fast that she felt she would topple over and at that point she would dive forward, arms outstretched. But instead of falling, instead of plummeting to the ground in a heap, B would swoop upwards with the grace and ease of a swift and soar high into the sky. Up she would glide, in great arcing sweeps over the countryside and with each turn, a wave of ecstasy would wash over her, and it was at that moment that the dream became lucid.

From that point in the dream, B could determine where and how she flew; she was in complete control. The slightest manipulation of her hands or tilt of her fingers would expertly adjust her pitch and altitude. Her exhilaration intensified as she swooped downwards and sped over the wild grass meadows – her fingertips brushing the tips of the blades as she sped silently above. All the while, the sun bathed her in glorious warmth. In those moments within the dream, she felt blessed and highly favoured. She felt her purpose was certain and her path was clear. At that moment in the dream, the sun would shine with extraordinary brightness and a blanket of brilliant white light would bring B back to a wakened state of energised calm and reflection.

Through their daily talks, B's friendship with Lina blossomed further. There was never any pretence or any agenda; there was only ever openness, transparency, and cooperation. This was a relationship based on authentic love and mutual respect. Every time they spoke, they learnt a little bit more about each other, and their connected universe expanded.

Lina knew that the forest had not yet revealed all its secrets to B. 'I have something you must see,' she said. 'Let's go.'

It was a Sunday morning. The temperature was particularly mild and as they set out into the forest, Lina took even more time and care than usual to point out the wondrous details of the flora and fauna.

Lina paused at the edge of the forest where an abundance of orchids grew. Intricate bell-shaped flowers in dazzling hues of magenta radiated vibrancy and vivacity. Lina beckoned B a little closer. 'Come,' she called. 'Stand very, very still.'

Sure enough, within seconds, the air around B's ears

buzzed with activity - a hummingbird, as small as B's little finger, hovered with perfect precision and began feeding on the nectar within the orchids. B's eyes lit up in surprise and awe. She looked to Lina who was smiling broadly. Lina gave a little nod as if to say, 'I know!'

Then a second hummingbird arrived, slightly larger than the first; its ruby red throat feathers flashed with shimmering iridescence. The two birds flitted between the flowers with such finesse that B was utterly entranced – the stillness of their heads, the fineness of their bills and their glistening bead-like eyes had her transfixed.

'Vámonos,' Lina whispered and gestured softly for B to follow her.

They walked deep into the forest and for the entire time Lina didn't say a word. Then without warning, she silently came to a halt a few feet in front of B, turned and said, 'I have been very excited to bring you here.' With that, she stepped off the trail and headed off into the thick, unchartered centre of the forest. Within a second, Lina had disappeared and so, with a little pang of panic in her chest, B followed her.

Lina moved with a quiet, assured speed and yet her every step was sympathetic to the forest. B, trailing a little way behind, felt like a toddler in comparison – stumbling and tripping in her wake. Even now, after weeks in the forest, she was not accustomed to the uneven, busy forest floor where the hazards were numerous and camouflaged.

On they walked, deeper and deeper into the heart of the forest. B had never been this far off the trails. The vegetation was so dense that it was easy to become disorientated and to lose one's way entirely, even within the space of a few steps. Indeed, they'd walked so far that B began to wonder if Lina knew where they were heading. But just then, as if she were reading B's mind, Lina turned and simply said, 'Nearly there.' And sure enough, within a few minutes Lina came to a stop.

And there it was.

'The Mother Tree,' Lina said and with an open hand she beckoned B forward as if presenting the most incredible gift. And indeed, it was.

The Mother Tree was so large and so majestic that for a moment B could neither move nor speak. She felt immensely grateful just to be able to see it. She stepped towards the enormous tree and began to lift her arm to touch the vast trunk, but she stopped herself just before her hand made contact. She turned and looked to Lina as if to seek permission. Lina laughed. 'Of course! Of course! You don't have to ask me! This tree belongs to no-one!' Lina laughed again before adding, 'We belong with it B! All things belong with it!'

B placed her hand against the bark of the ancient tree. Then she raised the palm of her other hand and placed it there too. Instantly, she felt grounded. A surge of positive energy flowed in and through her.

And then something happened that B did not expect and could not explain: the tree spoke to her. Not in words. Not in language. The communication was ineffable and yet B understood exactly what was being said, she felt it. The tree spoke of trust and love and safety. It whispered, 'All things worth knowing are found within. To know the world, you do not need to seek, you do not need to strive, you only need to look within.'

B did not know how long she had been standing there – it might've been thirty seconds or thirty minutes – but it was only when Lina said, 'Come. Come. We're not done here,' that she realised how deep in trance she had been.

Lina led B around the great tree. It was many, many metres in circumference. Lina told her that it once took eight people, all with their arms outstretched and hands linked, to wrap all the way around the tree. And that, she said, had been many years ago when they first arrived at the forest.

Lina paused, turned to B and with a glint in her eye gave a nod of her head towards the ground. With that, Lina bent right down, almost to her hands and knees, and squeezing through a narrow opening in the trunk disappeared inside the colossal tree.

Once again, B was so astonished that for a moment she was entirely frozen. She looked around her into the forest, looked down at the opening in the tree trunk, and then she too stooped down and edged forward into the dark interior of the Mother Tree.

B fumbled around blindly while her eyes adjusted to the darkness. Lina guided her in, and B gripped her hand tightly for reassurance.

'It's ok. It's ok,' Lina whispered softly. 'Here, sit. Sit.'

The two women sat with their backs against the inside of the trunk. B hugged her knees against her chest. Gradually her eyes began to adjust, and she could make out her surroundings; the space inside the tree was huge. It was warm, surprisingly so, and dry too. A small glow of light entered through the opening.

'This is the Mother Tree,' said Lina. And for a long, long time the two women sat in silence.

Crease by crease, B felt the worry that had been etched on her face melt away. Muscle by muscle, the tension held in her body dissipated. Her breath slowed and her heartbeat followed suit. Her knees lowered to the sides and her hands rested upon her legs.

B felt the age of the tree. Its ancient roots spread far and deep through the forest floor. Its thick branches reached high and wide across the canopy. The roots, in darkness, bringing security and life-giving water. The leaves, honouring the sky above, harnessing the light, providing life-giving oxygen for all. B understood the balance. The forest was alive, was life itself, and yet it was inexorably held in the grip of death - she herself sat in the dying heart of the mother.

In her mind's eye, B saw the entire lifespan of the Mother Tree play out. From germinating seed to vulnerable sapling to maturing oak, strong and dominant, to ancient

Mother Tree, right through to its eventual demise – dying, cracking, falling, decomposing back into the forest floor from whence it arose. A thousand years played out in mere seconds; B saw it all. She saw the acorns that the Mother Tree had dropped, and the saplings that grew up from them and though some perished, many prospered and bore their own seeds. And so, the forest grew, and it thrived. B saw the cycle of the sun and Earth. She saw the Mother Tree living and dying under the light of a hundred thousand sunrises. Its permanence an illusion. Its life just a heartbeat, before returning to the forest floor to provide for and foster new life - completing the cycle. Perfect unity. Not through action. Not through desire. No will. Only being something, for some time and then being something else. Not disappearing but changing. Not dying but transforming. Only transforming.

OPPORTUNITIES

(Things you might do for yourself)

- So often, it is not our fear of death that prevents us realising our dreams but our fear of life. It is our fear of the risk, our fear of failure and sometimes our fear of success that pulls us back. By knowing and accepting that life and death are two sides of the same coin, we can begin to free ourselves of their power over us. Remind yourself that we are only something, for some time and then we are not that thing, we are becoming and being something else. The one question we must ask ourselves while we are being this thing is: *How* do you want to be it? Write down your dreams and wishes – write down what could be if you had no fears pulling you back. How does your dream life compare with your actual existence now?

AFFIRMATIONS

(Things you might say to yourself)

- All things worth knowing are found within.

- To know the world, I must look inside myself.

SELF REFLECTION

(Things you might ask yourself)

- Is it time for you to take control of your life? Are you awake to your potential? Or are you sleepwalking through everyday life? Are you clambering up the hill on all fours or are you ready to fly your own course? Are you ready to transform?

12 TRUST

It was twilight by the time B and Lina left the Mother Tree. The lack of light penetrating through to the forest floor caught B off guard; she was dazed and fuzzy.

The forest, usually a panoply of greens was cast into thinning greyness. Monotone.

The whole world seemed to be stumbling sideways as day slipped away into night.

As they set off to head home, B reached her arm forward and placed her hand on Lina's shoulder. Lina turned and with her usual calm, quiet assuredness said, 'It's ok. I know the way. And the path knows me.'

Within a matter of moments, any remnants of daylight had vanished. The darkness was a thick blanket and B was walking blindly. Earlier she had stumbled in Lina's wake but now she was utterly helpless. In that moment she could feel her own vulnerability and it made her laugh. B reached out and once again placed her hand upon Lina's shoulder. 'I need you to guide me!' she said to Lina.

'No. You only think you do.' came Lina's reply. 'Soon you won't need me at all.'

Despite Lina's assertion, B needed her very much. The darkness of a forest at night is unlike any other kind of darkness you will experience. It is closed, cloying, restrictive and yet simultaneously vast, all pervading and limitless. It is capable of inducing fear and liberation in equal measure.

For Lina, it was always the latter that came to the fore and so, feeling the dark's familiar embrace she began to hum. The tune was a lullaby her mother had sung to her and her brothers - it was slow and calming. The vibration reverberated through Lina's ribcage, through her shoulder and into the palm and fingertips of B's hand. Once again, B could see outside herself, she could see the pair of them – her traipsing blindly whilst being led by the humming, wise lady of the forest. And once again, she laughed out loud.

'Now why do you laugh?' asked Lina.

'I'm laughing at us! At this!' replied B. 'I don't think anyone, anywhere in the world, is doing this right now! Do you?'

Lina let out a little snort of delight. 'No, I don't suppose they are!' she replied. And the two of them laughed and hummed together.

The laughter and humming had swept away B's thoughts and worries. What use were they anyway? Earlier, her thoughts had coming racing at her – scattergun and incessant. What use was that to her? Her thoughts had dictated her state – she was scared, and she worried about tripping and falling in the dark. When? In the future. Worrying constantly about the 'what if.' Her anxiety did not assist her, did not show her the way. On the contrary, her thoughts distracted her. What use were they?

Now, as the thoughts came, B consciously let them pass away. The rapid-fire assault slowed to an occasional pop. The worry came, B let it pass – it was no use to her.

Now as she walked, the ground beneath her came to meet the exact alignment of her footsteps. The tree roots that jutted into the trail now fell in the natural rhythm of her gait so that she effortlessly stepped over them. Her head swayed naturally out of the way of overhanging branches so that the leaves just brushed her hair as she passed beneath.

The path that she had passed over was gone. The path ahead was untrodden. There was only the path she was on; every step she took was in the present. Thoughts came and she let them pass – they were just something that had been for some time, and now they were something else.

B took her hand from Lina's shoulder.

'You don't need me now?' asked Lina.

'Ha! Not so much!' came B's reply and the two of them walked on in silence, in the dark of the ancient forest.

OPPORTUNITIES

(Things you might do for yourself)

- We all need guidance. From time to time, no matter how independent we are, we need to accept that the experience, skills, and knowledge of others can benefit us. To accept help is not a weakness, it is a strength. Be guided. Follow in the footsteps of others but know that the best guides are those that understand when it is time to allow the follower to tread their own path.

AFFIRMATIONS

(Things you might say to yourself)

- The past serves no purpose – I do not dwell there.

- To future is an illusion therefore I do not fear or desire it.

- There is only the present. All I do and all I am, is now.

SELF REFLECTION

(Things you might ask yourself)

- How often are you consumed by your thoughts? To what extent do your own thoughts dictate your actions or sabotage them? Beware your thoughts – they aren't as useful as you imagine. Be aware of your thoughts - let them pass through without attachment.

13 BALANCE

Emerging from the forest, B and Lina were greeted by a night sky that was as startlingly clear as it was beautiful.

'Ah!' exclaimed Lina, almost as if she was seeing this wondrous sky or the very first time. 'Now, we must stargaze!'

They returned to the cabin, fetched blankets, snacks and hot chocolate and set out again, Lina led them up the hillside to a clearing just off the track. They picked their spot, unfurled their blankets, and laid down under the glory of the night sky.

If you ever need to reassure yourself of your place in the universe, then travel to the Talamanca Mountains in the Central Valley region of Costa Rica. Wait for a clear night, pitch up a warm blanket and a makeshift pillow, lay down and gaze upwards. The altitude, the clarity and purity of the air, and the absence of any light pollution contribute to a faultless view of the stars above. The Milky Way arcs over you almost within touch; a brooding, sweeping cloud of stars that is monumental and majestic and yet subtle and silent in its magnificence.

As B lay staring, she was confronted by her own insignificance. More precisely, she felt the insignificance of her identity, her persona, her thoughts, and her own emotions. More precisely still, she came to the realisation that she *was* significant but that everything else was equally significant. In that moment, B felt that the blade of grass that brushed against the side of her hand had the same significance as the stars above her and that she was as significant as both - but no more and no less.

The grass and the stars sought nothing and thought nothing; they just were. They were something for some time and they would become something else. Stars. Eyes. Grass. Skin. All of them majestic and monumental.

OPPORTUNITIES

(Things you might do for yourself)

- You must create opportunities for yourself to look up, look out and look beyond. Too often in our daily lived experiences we encounter the familiar because we are creatures of comfort, routine, and habit. You must break out of your norm. You must seize every available opportunity to push back the familiar, break out the routines and burst the bubble of familiarity that we surround ourselves with. The night sky is the perfect place to start. Go nightwalking. Go stargazing. Look beyond.

AFFIRMATIONS

(Things you might say to yourself)

- I am significant.

- My place is here. My time is now.

SELF REFLECTION

(Things you might ask yourself)

- How much of our lives are consumed by seeking and gaining significance? How often do we equate status or wealth or success with purpose and meaning? If we achieve those things, are we more significant? The stars do not strive for status or wealth, are they any less significant for not achieving them?

14 REDISCOVER

The longer B spent in the forest, the more confident she became in exploring it fully. She pursued the creation of the new purple trail diligently but at the end of each day she would make a point of walking off-trail to make her way home. The idea of intentionally losing herself would previously have filled B with anxiety and doubt but now she relished it as an opportunity.

And every day she made sure to walk to the forest edge and bathe in the clouds as they breezed in across the valley and swept in amongst the trees. And that point every day, she would lay her palm on the trunk of a tree and still herself. She would acknowledge any thoughts that came into her mind and then she would let them waft away with the clouds. She would listen to the tree, and it would speak to her about its roots below and its branches above. The tree did not seek, it only was.

On one such day, B walked out to the edge of the forest, immersed herself in the clouds as normal but then, instead of turning back into the forest to return home, she set out to explore. Skirting the edge of the forest, she climbed upwards towards the mountain's peak. She climbed and climbed, higher than she had ever been before.

B came to rest at a little plateau that gave her the most spectacular vista of her surroundings. She stood, arms by her side, relaxed and calm and simply soaked in the views. To her left and below her, B could see the cabins and the whole swathe of Lina's cloud forest. Looking out ahead of her, the valley lay like an open book. She could see the tiny huts and homesteads dotted on the snaking tracks. And there was the river, a spine running the length of the valley, twisting out of sight around the knuckles of the mountain.

Above her, the sky was that white, light blue that masterpieces are made of - clear and pristine.

And bursting life and light on it all, high and to the west, was the sun. Its warmth all-pervading. Its light energising life, firing cells, and driving the cycle of photosynthesis.

Air and light and water and trees. B felt part of it all. She felt connected. Her breath slowed. The warmth of the sun kissed the skin of her face and embraced her body. She had the sensation of becoming lighter as if the effect of gravity on her was lessened, just fractionally. It was if some unknown weight she had been carrying was lifted off her.

She closed her eyes and the light and warmth intensified. B smiled. She had felt this warmth before – it was the same warmth she had experienced falling into her altered state as a child, while dozing in the long grass. The feeling of blissful wakefulness intensified further still.

As B stood on the mountainside, she closed her eyes and began to feel happiness surge within her. The light and warmth flowed into her chest. B could feel it pouring into her, so much so that she felt that she could actually touch it – a stream of pure light pulsing into her heart.

Then came a realisation that this light felt like pure love. Yes, B felt like this light was love. A flow of energy rushing into her body bringing love-light resonating in her heart. And her body filled with it, like water filling a cup. B felt the energy flow in and through her. And the more it flowed, the more B felt her experience expanding. She felt herself, her thoughts, her consciousness expanding vastly outwards across the valley, and then up and outwards across the sky. And on it went, up and out, up and out, across space and across time. On it went, expanding outwards until B was connected to all things, across all time.

The light, the energy, the love that connected to and with B spoke to her. What it said cannot be communicated in words. It cannot be known only experienced. It is ineffable and beyond description. But if she had to, if she could, B might say that in those brief moments, the energy shared with her the knowledge that everything and every time is utterly and incontrovertibly connected; one and the same. B might say that the love and the light and the energy transcend space and time. They flow in all things, at all times. And she might say that being is transient, but connection is permanent. That every thing, living and non-living, is significant and sacred.

B was fizzing with certainty and contentedness. She had an overwhelming feeling of reassurance and comfort. Everything was as it should be. Everything was moving through her, supporting her and she in turn was supporting everything else because they were one and the same. To know herself was to know everything. And underlying all things was love – a universal, pure love that was wholly shared.

Although it felt much longer, this state of blissful connection lasted no than twenty or thirty minutes. As it began to subside, B opened her eyes. She felt total harmony and contentedness within her. Every cell, every atom, every particle of her existence vibrated with a glow of certainty and assuredness that she had never known before. Waves of energy and warmth pulsated through her.

Looking around, she was able to discern the energy of every living thing around her: the grass, the trees, the ground itself, all glowed with the same energy. B crouched down to brush her hand through the grass. Only, she didn't touch the grass itself, instead she brushed through the energy that was surrounding and running through it; her own energy effortlessly melded and connected with it, like fingers trailing through a gentle stream.

B stood up and once again took in the steep slope of the mountainside that ran downwards beneath her. She smiled, took a step forward and then another and another. She began to trot and then to run, running faster and faster until she was hurtling down the slope. Head forward, she ran faster, and faster, until she felt her feet couldn't keep up and she would certainly tumble over and at that very moment, she flung her arms forward and dived into the air. But to her shock, B did not come crashing down to the earth, instead she kept diving outwards over the valley. B smiled and then laughed. With confidence and absolute certainty, she stretched her arms out to her sides, like the unfurling of magnificent wings, and with that she soared up, up into the big blue of the open sky. Whooping with joy, B flew high and then swooped down in great arcs over the valley. She swept over the tops of the trees of Lina's cloud forest. From here she could see everything – the cabins, the trails, and even the Mother Tree. She was the Resplendent Quetzal – her own spirit bird. She was the air. She was the sun. She was the light. She was the clouds. She was free.

OPPORTUNITIES
(Things you might do for yourself)

- You must begin to realise that you are capable of great things. You are capable of whatever you dream of. You are capable of breaking free of the bounds that tie you to your current lived experience. The light of the universe is within you. The energy of all things connects to and through you. To discover the true nature of all things you must first look inside yourself. If you yearn for more, then you must begin your exploration today. In order to give yourself space to explore inside, you must start outside – the natural world is you. Start there. Start today.

AFFIRMATIONS
(Things you might say to yourself)

- I am light. I am energy. I am love.
- Everything is connected. We are all one and the same.
- Time is an illusion. There is only now.

SELF REFLECTION
(Things you might ask yourself)

- What does your gut tell you about the nature of all things? What does your heart tell you about your connection with nature? Isn't it time for you to trust your own feelings and make the change you know to be right?

15 THE TIME AFTER

When B returned to the cabin that evening, she relayed the extraordinary events of the afternoon to Lina. Lina, quite unfazed by the tale and with her characteristic calm, offered B a very short and simple explanation: 'That's why you came here,' she said as if it were the most obvious of facts.

B spent the remainder of her time at the forest completing the purple trail. She worked incredibly hard and was rightly proud of it. It sympathetically meandered through the forest, taking its cue from the established trees and the terrain.

On her very last day in the forest, B went alone to explore one final time. She wandered on and off the trails. She walked in the clouds and connected with the mighty trees. All the while, the afterglow of her experience on the mountainside remained within her body and soul. She felt a serenity unlike any calmness she had felt before; she was deeply secure in her place and her purpose. She felt totally at ease with who she was and in complete harmony with the world around her. The forest seemed to hum with the soft reverberation of energy. B was tuned in to it and it confirmed to her that she was inextricably connected to all things.

B sat at the base of an enormous laurel. The silence of the forest was a welcome friend. She felt enormously grateful to be there and to be part of the incredible ecosystem. Then, as if to say a final farewell, the forest had one last surprise to offer her. Above her head, she heard the unmistakeable sound of flapping wings. Looking up, B was astonished to witness a Resplendent Quetzal landing on a branch no more than twenty feet above her. The bird's green plumage sparkled like an emerald of unrivalled magnificence, and the red of its breast feathers seared through the forest like lava. B could not believe her luck. If she had felt grateful before, now she felt truly blessed; the sight of the regal bird was a gift beyond compare. The Quetzal's stay was fleeting and after some self-preening, it took flight and was gone. B took that as her cue to leave and for the very last time she headed out of the cloud forest back to Lina's cabin.

Saying goodbye to Lina was difficult and emotional. The two women had bonded in a way that neither of them could've imagined. They cried and hugged, and then they laughed at the fact that they were crying, and they hugged again. Then Lina insisted that Higuel take a photograph of them – which by all accounts was a very rare request.

Finally, it was time to leave. Lina had made B a little pack lunch of her favourite snacks and had arranged for a friend to drive B across the valley up to the main road to meet the bus. As she drove away, juddering this way and that on the bumpy track, B looked back in the mirror to see Lina waving goodbye. A second later, the truck turned the corner, and she was gone. Tears welled up in B's eyes and then rolled in great streams down her cheeks.

B spent the next couple of months exploring Costa Rica. She took buses here and hitchhiked there. She travelled coast to coast visiting the volcanoes, and the waterfalls and the impeccable beaches.

B went where her heart took her, as if she was floating

on the breeze. She was light - carrying no angst or concern. She was natural - pure and loving. She was in balance - harmonious and connected. She sought nothing. She was something for some time and then she was something else. She was free. She was herself.

Printed in Great Britain
by Amazon

22192103R00051